FlashKids

SKILLS

Reading Comprehension

Written by **Michelle Thompson**

Illustrated by **Jackie Snider**

FlashKids

New York

This book belongs to

_____

New York

An Imprint of Sterling Publishing Co., Inc.
33 East 17th Street
New York, NY 10003

FLASH KIDS and the distinctive Flash Kids logo are registered trademarks of
Barnes and Noble, Inc.

Text and illustrations © 2006 Flash Kids

This edition of READING COMPREHENSION: GRADE 2 published in 2024 by
Sterling Publishing Co., Inc.

ISBN 978-1-4114-8075-9

For information about custom editions, special sales, and premium
purchases, please contact specialsales@unionsquareandco.com.

Printed in Malaysia

Lot #:
2 4 6 8 10 9 7 5 3 1
09/23

unionsquareandco.com

Cover illustration: Justin Poulter; cover design: Melissa Farris

Dear Grown-up,

Once young children have learned to read, the next important step is to make sure that they understand and retain the information they encounter. The passages and activities contained in this book will provide your child with plenty of opportunities to develop these vital reading comprehension skills. The more your child reads and responds to literature, the greater the improvement you will see in their mastery of reading comprehension. To get the most from this book, follow these simple steps:

- Find a comfortable place where you and your child can work quietly together.

- Encourage your child to work at their own pace.

- Help your child read the words and sentences, and ask questions about the content of what they have read.

- Offer lots of praise and support.

- Let your child reward their work with the included stickers.

- Most of all, remember that learning should be fun! Take time to look at the pictures, laugh at the funny characters, and enjoy this special time spent together.

Birthday Breakfast

Early Saturday morning, the smell of bacon cooking woke Peter from his sleep. He jumped out of bed. He grabbed his robe and put it on over his pajamas. He ran downstairs to the kitchen. "Surprise!" shouted his family. They were all waiting around the table to wish Peter a happy birthday.

Fill in the blanks to the clues below. Write the answers in the puzzle.

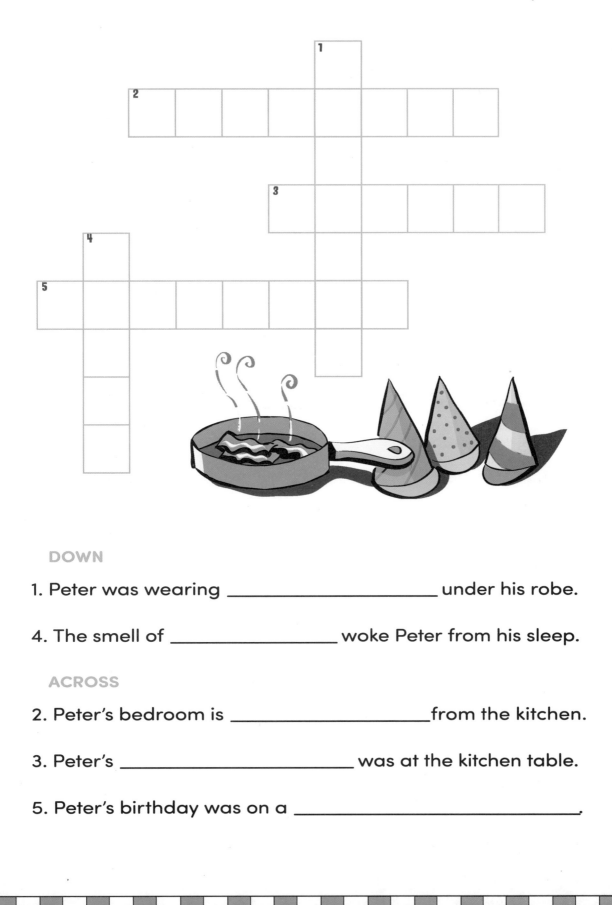

DOWN

1. Peter was wearing _____ under his robe.

4. The smell of _____ woke Peter from his sleep.

ACROSS

2. Peter's bedroom is _____from the kitchen.

3. Peter's _____ was at the kitchen table.

5. Peter's birthday was on a _____.

Helping Hands

Lending a helping hand is a great way to let your family know that you care. There are many things that you can do to pitch in. One thing you can do is make your bed every day. You can also pick up your clothes and toys. At dinnertime, you can set the table or help clear the dishes. You can also help with daily chores, such as taking out the trash or sorting the laundry.

Answer the questions.

1. What are 3 things you can do to help around the house?

   _____

   _____

   _____

2. What is one example of a daily chore?

   _____

3. When you lend a helping hand, what does it tell your family about you?

   _____

   _____

   _____

   _____

Butterfly Life Cycle

Caterpillars are small insects that hatch from eggs. In the first part of their lives, they crawl on the ground and on trees. They eat leaves for food. Then they form cocoons, where they sleep for a long time. Inside the cocoons, they start to change. When they come out of the cocoons, they have turned into beautiful butterflies! This amazing process is called the life cycle of the butterfly.

Number the life-cycle stages in order according to the story.

_____   _____

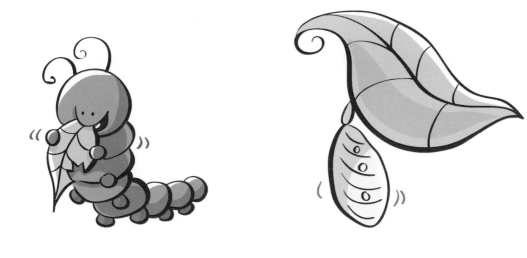

_____   _____

9

Uncle Miguel

Everyone loves Uncle Miguel! When he comes to visit, he brings toys for each of the children. He plays hide-and-seek with us. He shows us how to make silly faces and do magic tricks. Uncle Miguel tells funny stories that make everyone roar with laughter. When Uncle Miguel is around, everyone is happy!

Read each statement. Write true or false.

1. No one likes Uncle Miguel. _____

2. Uncle Miguel can do magic tricks. _____

3. Uncle Miguel makes fun of children. _____

4. Uncle Miguel plays hide-and-seek. _____

5. Uncle Miguel tells funny stories. _____

Going to Grandma's

Mandy was very excited! She was packing her suitcase to go visit her grandma for the weekend. Mandy folded her clothes and put them neatly into the bag. Then she packed 2 pairs of shoes. Mandy added her toothbrush and comb. She thought about packing a game, but then she remembered that Grandma had a lot of games to play at her house. Finally, Mandy placed her stuffed elephant on top of the pile of clothes and zipped her suitcase. She was ready to go!

Answer the questions using the information from the story.

1. How did Mandy feel about visiting her grandma's

   house?

   _____

2. Which items did Mandy pack in her suitcase?
   Circle the items.

Fishing Trip

Sarah opened the can of worms. She carefully lifted a worm out of the dirt-filled can. The worm wiggled to get free, but Sarah held on tightly. She grabbed the hook between her fingers. Then she quickly slid the worm onto the hook. Sarah cast her line into the pond and waited to catch a fish.

Number the events in the story in the order in which they happen.

_____ Sarah put the worm onto the hook.

_____ The worm wiggled to get free.

_____ Sarah waited to catch a fish.

_____ Sarah opened the can of worms.

_____ Sarah cast her line into the pond.

_____ Sarah lifted the worm out of the can.

Safety Rules

A police officer came to our school to talk to us about safety. She reminded us to wear our helmets while riding bicycles and buckle our seatbelts while riding in cars. She told us that we should always look both ways before crossing the street to make sure traffic is clear. The police officer said it is important for us to follow these safety rules so that we don't get hurt.

Fill in the blanks to the clues below. Write the answers in the puzzle.

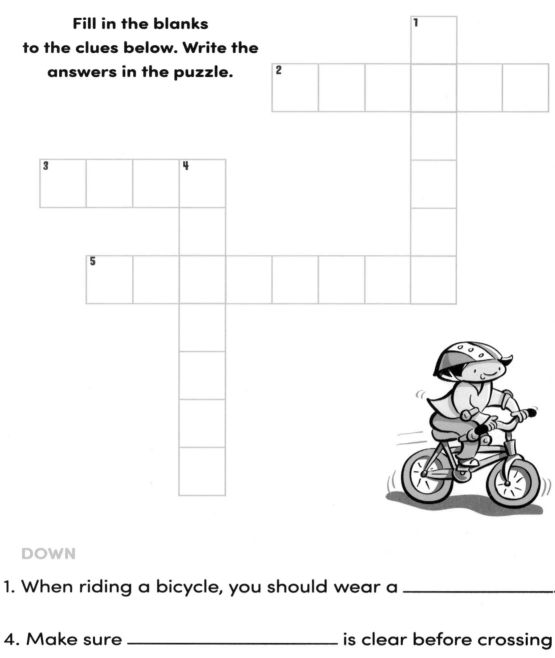

DOWN

1. When riding a bicycle, you should wear a _____.

4. Make sure _____ is clear before crossing

   the street.

ACROSS

2. The police officer talked to the students about _____.

3. Follow safety rules so that you don't get _____.

5. You should put on a _____ when riding in a car.

Origami Art

Origami is the Japanese art of folding square pieces of paper to make different-shaped objects, such as birds, flowers, and fish. In fact, the word *origami* means "to fold paper." Origami is a very old tradition enjoyed by both young and old. Surprisingly, no glue or scissors are needed. Once completed, the finished product is often a beautifully decorative creation.

Answer the questions.

1. What does the word *origami* mean?

   _____

2. What are some shapes that can be made using
   origami?

   _____

   _____

3. What supplies are needed to make origami?

   _____

4. Which culture does origami come from?

   _____

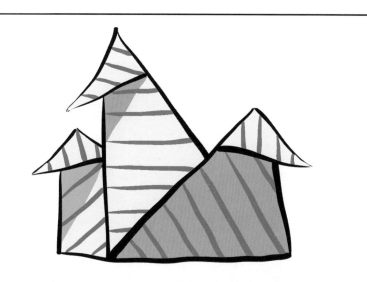

S'mores

Have you ever eaten s'mores around a campfire? To make s'mores, you place a marshmallow on a stick and roast it over an open fire. You place the marshmallow on a graham cracker with a small piece of chocolate. Then you sandwich the marshmallow by placing another graham cracker on top. Finally, you eat it! S'mores may seem like a funny name for food, but this tasty treat got its name because people who ate it were always asking for "some more!"

Fill in the blanks with the correct answer.

1. Most people eat s'mores around a _____.

2. To make s'mores, you need to place a marshmallow

   on a _____.

3. Then, you hold the marshmallow over the fire to

   _____ it.

4. S'mores are made of marshmallows, graham crackers,

   and _____.

5. The name s'mores was created by people asking

   for _____ _____.

The Great Lakes

There are 5 bodies of water along the northern border of the United States. They are known as the Great Lakes. They are called Lake Huron, Lake Ontario, Lake Michigan, Lake Erie, and Lake Superior. The Great Lakes hold about 6 quadrillion gallons of water! These lakes provide most of our country's fresh water supply.

Answer the questions.

1. Along which border of the United States are the Great Lakes?

   _____

2. How many gallons of water do the Great Lakes hold?

   _____

3. Find and circle the names of the 5 Great Lakes in the word search below.

E R A T M V

A M V B E H Y T O N E

L I M L E M O K C W S

G C H U R O N Q U X C

M H N E I Y T S K P J

F I J B E C A M V L H

I G M K Z S R L N P W

M A M I C H I G A N R

S U P E R I O R S U E

Spiders and Insects

Some people think that spiders are insects, but they are not. Insects have only 6 legs, but spiders have 8. Insects have 3 body parts: the head, the thorax, and the abdomen. Spiders have only 2 body parts because their head and thorax are fused together. Spiders can have as many as 8 eyes, but insects only have 2. Unlike insects, spiders do not have wings.

Fill in the chart.

	SPIDERS	INSECTS
Number of legs:		
Number of body parts:		
Do they have fused heads and thoraxes?		
Number of eyes:		
Do they have wings?		

The White House

The White House is home to the President of the United States. Located in Washington, D.C., at 1600 Pennsylvania Avenue, the White House has 132 rooms, 35 bathrooms, 8 staircases, and 3 elevators! The first president to live inside this huge home was President John Adams. Since that time, each new president and First Family have resided in the White House. It is sometimes called the Executive Mansion or the President's Palace.

Answer the questions.

1. Who lives in the White House?

   _____

2. What is the address of the White House?

   _____

3. How many bathrooms are in the White House?

   _____

4. Who was the first president to live in the White House?

   _____

5. What are other names for the White House?

   _____

   _____

Juggling

Have you ever wanted to learn how to juggle? All you need are 3 small beanbags and a lot of practice. First, hold 1 beanbag in each hand. Toss 1 beanbag in a high arc in front of your body toward the other hand. While the first beanbag is in the air, pass the second beanbag from one hand to the other. Then catch the first beanbag with your free hand. Once you practice this over and over again, add a third beanbag! Soon, you will be juggling!

Number the events in order.

_____ Pass the second beanbag
from one hand to the other.

_____ Hold 1 beanbag
in each hand.

_____ Toss 1 beanbag in a high
arc toward the other hand.

_____ Add a third beanbag.

_____ Catch the first beanbag
with your free hand.

Lovely Ladybugs

Ladybugs are very interesting insects to observe. When they fly, ladybugs beat their wings 85 times in one second! You won't see them flying around in cold weather, though, because ladybugs won't fly in temperatures below 55 degrees Fahrenheit. Unlike people, ladybugs chew their food from side to side, not up and down. Even though they won't hurt you, they can sometimes bite . . . so please don't bother them!

Read each statement. Write true or false.

1. Ladybugs beat their wings 65 times per second. _____

2. Ladybugs won't fly in cold weather. _____

3. Ladybugs chew their food in the same way that people do. _____

4. Ladybugs can bite. _____

5. A bite from a ladybug is very painful. _____

Greeting Cards

Have you ever received a birthday card in the mail? The custom of mailing greeting cards began in Great Britain over 150 years ago. In 1840, the British government passed a law that lowered the cost of mail delivery. In 1843, a British businessman, Henry Cole, hired an artist to design a greeting card. He sold it to people to send through the mail. The greeting card contained the message "A Merry Christmas and a Happy New Year to You." Today, people can buy greeting cards for many different occasions, including birthdays, Valentine's Day, Mother's Day, and other holidays!

Answer the questions.

1. Where did the custom of mailing greeting cards begin?

   _____

2. In what year did the British government lower the cost of mail delivery?

   _____

3. Who was the businessman who began the greeting card business?

   _____

4. What message did the first greeting card contain?

   _____

   _____

5. Name an occasion for which you can buy a greeting card.

   _____

   _____

   _____

Underwater Animals

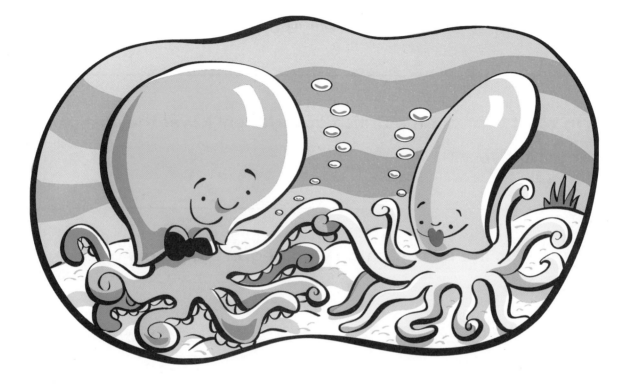

An octopus and a squid are two kinds of animals that live in the ocean. An octopus has 8 arms, with hundreds of suckers that allow it to move along in the ocean. An octopus feeds on crab, lobster, and other shellfish. A squid has 8 arms and 2 tentacles and enjoys eating fish, some shellfish, and other squid.

Use the facts below to fill in the Venn diagram.
The first one is done for you.

FACTS:

Eats other squid   Lives in the ocean

Has 8 arms   Has 8 arms and 2 tentacles

Eats fish   Has hundreds of suckers

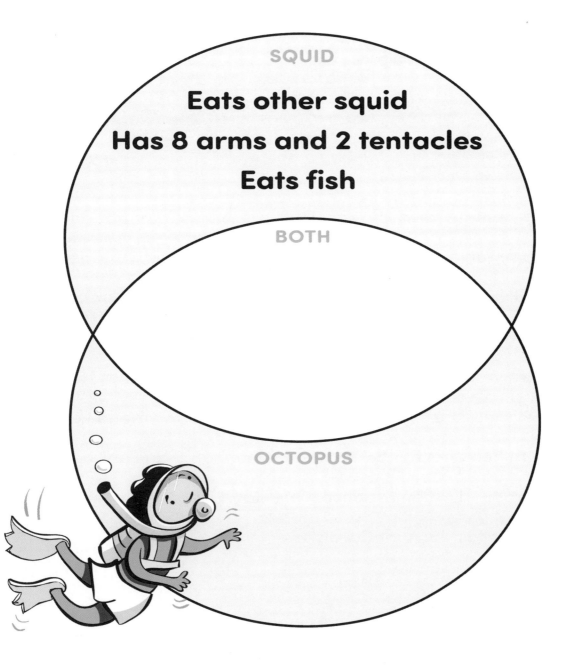

SQUID

Eats other squid
Has 8 arms and 2 tentacles
Eats fish

BOTH

OCTOPUS

American Sign Language

My Aunt Carolyn is deaf. That means she cannot hear. To communicate with her, my family learned American Sign Language, or ASL. When we want to communicate with Aunt Carolyn, we use our hands to sign the words that we want to say. She uses her hands to sign back to us. Sometimes, she signs so fast that it is hard for me to keep up with her. I have a book about American Sign Language in my room so I can practice. One day, I hope I will be able to sign as fast as Aunt Carolyn.

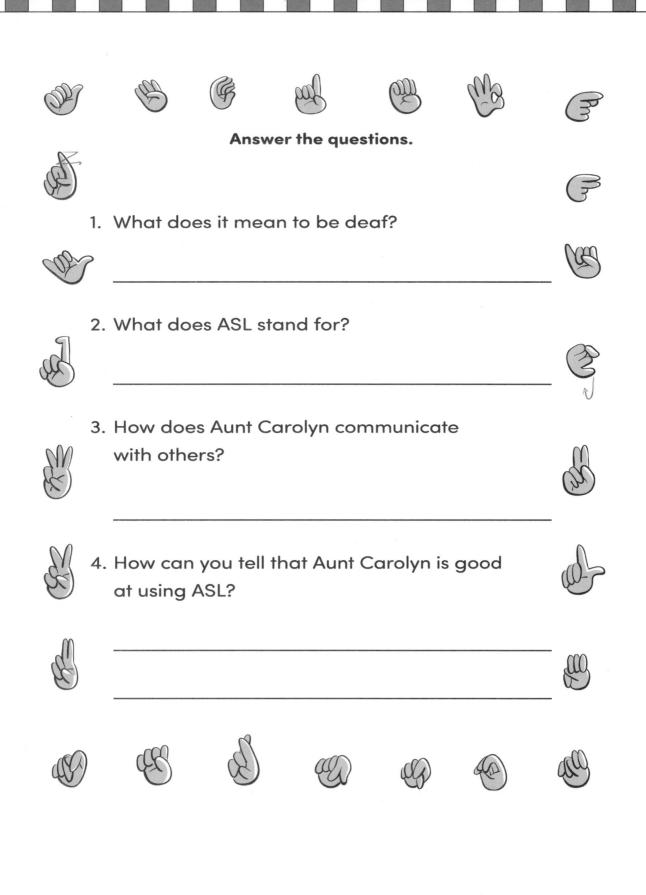

Answer the questions.

1. What does it mean to be deaf?

   _____

2. What does ASL stand for?

   _____

3. How does Aunt Carolyn communicate
   with others?

   _____

4. How can you tell that Aunt Carolyn is good
   at using ASL?

   _____

   _____

Navajo Tradition

Ever since she was a little girl, Sasha has watched her mother and grandmother make beautiful rugs out of wool. As part of the Navajo nation, Sasha's family passes this tradition on from one generation to the next. Sasha helps to clean, spin, and dye the wool before it is ready to go on the loom. Soon, Sasha will learn how to weave patterns herself so that she may one day pass this part of her culture on to the next generation.

Read each statement. Write true or false.

1. Sasha is teaching her grandmother how to weave. _____

2. Navajo rugs are made of silk. _____

3. Sasha is part of the Navajo nation. _____

4. The wool of a rug is dyed after the rug is completed. _____

5. Someday, Sasha will teach the next generation how to weave. _____

Firefighters

Firefighters are heroes in our communities. Their job is to fight fires and to rescue people in emergencies. When firefighters go to work, they often stay at the fire station for several days at a time. They sleep, eat, and exercise there with other firefighters who work in their station. When a fire bell sounds, the firefighters quickly grab their hats and gear, jump on the fire truck, and head to the scene of the fire. Once there, they use powerful fire hoses and extinguishers to put out fires. Every day, firefighters risk their lives to protect the safety of others.

Answer the questions.

1. What are two things that firefighters do in our communities?

   _____

   _____

2. What do firefighters do at the fire station?

   _____

3. When a fire bell sounds, what do firefighters take with them?

   _____

4. What are 2 tools that firefighters use to put out fires?

   _____

   _____

Veterinarians

Do you have a dog or cat? If so, you've probably taken your pet to visit a veterinarian. Veterinarians are doctors who care for animals instead of people. Veterinarians go to school for a long time to learn how to help animals of all kinds. Most veterinarians love animals and enjoy giving pet owners advice that will help their pets live happy and healthy lives.

Fill in the blanks to the clues below. Write the answers in the puzzle.

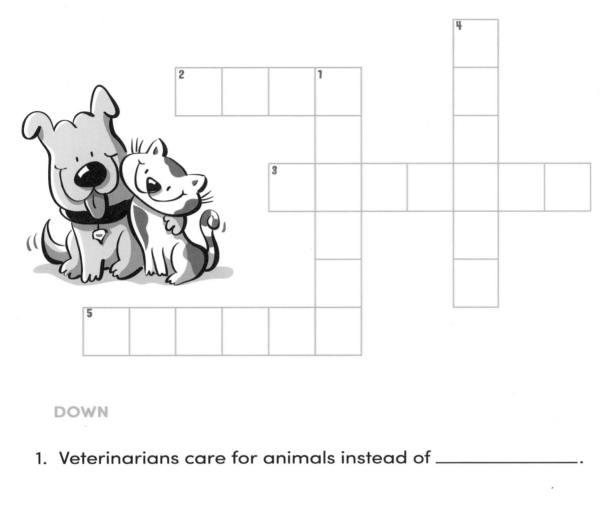

DOWN

1. Veterinarians care for animals instead of _____.

4. Veterinarians go to _____ to study for a long time.

ACROSS

2. Veterinarians _____ animals of all kinds.

3. Veterinarians are _____ who care for animals.

5. Veterinarians give _____ to pet owners.

Rainbows

Have you ever wondered what makes a rainbow? The colors of the rainbow are made by the sun's light reflecting off a sheet of water droplets in the sky. Once reflected inside the drops, the light bends in different directions and splits. Seven different colors can be seen. The colors always appear in this order: red, orange, yellow, green, blue, indigo, and violet. Next time you see a rainbow in the sky, you can tell a friend what caused it!

Circle the correct answer.

1. The colors of the rainbow are made by the sun's . . .

   a. heat   b. energy   c. light

2. The light is reflected off of a sheet of . . .

   a. blankets   b. water   c. linen

3. Inside the water droplets, the light is . . .

   a. split   b. bright   c. wet

4. The first color that appears in the rainbow is . . .

   a. green   b. orange   c. red

Draw a rainbow. Then color it, placing the colors in the correct order.

The Met

In 1870, a group of artists and businesspeople in New York City decided to create a place for art and art education. They opened the Metropolitan Museum of Art. The first piece of art in the museum was a carved Roman coffin. Today, the museum covers four city blocks and holds nearly 3 million valuable objects. Visitors can look at paintings, figures, pottery, and many other beautiful things. Every year, millions of people come to New York City to visit "the Met" and learn more about art.

Answer the questions.

1. Where is the Metropolitan Museum of Art?

    _____

2. What was the first piece of art in the museum?

    _____

3. How many objects are in the museum today?

    _____

4. What is a nickname for the Metropolitan Museum of Art?

    _____

Swimming Lessons

Brian is learning how to swim. He takes swimming lessons at the community pool every Monday and Wednesday afternoon. Before he started taking swimming lessons, Brian did not know how to swim at all. In fact, he was a little afraid of the water. Now, Brian enjoys swimming. So far, he has learned to do the backstroke, the crawl, and the sidestroke. Next week, Brian is going to jump off the diving board.

Answer the questions.

1. Where does Brian take swimming lessons?

   _____

2. When does Brian take swimming lessons?

   _____

3. Which 3 swimming strokes has Brian learned to do?

   _____

4. What will Brian do next week?

   _____

5. Do you think Brian is still afraid of the water? Explain.

   _____

   _____

   _____

   _____

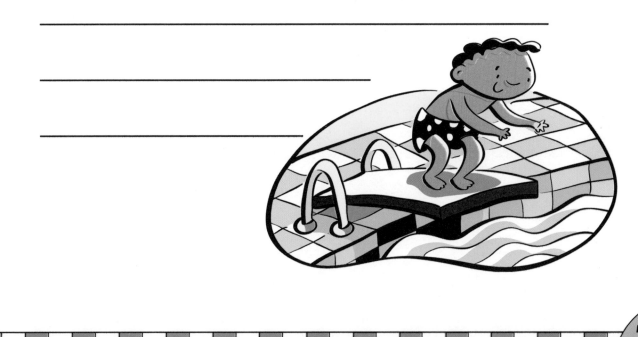

Birdhouse

Meghan bought a birdhouse from the garden store. She brought the birdhouse home and took it out of the box. Meghan hung the birdhouse from a tree branch in her backyard. She placed some birdseed in the bottom of the house. Then, Meghan sat on the porch and waited for the birds to fly into the birdhouse. Soon, birds were eating the seeds and chirping happily in Meghan's backyard.

Number the events in the order in which they happened.

_____ Meghan put birdseed in the house.

_____ Meghan bought a birdhouse from the store.

_____ Meghan sat on the porch and waited for the birds.

_____ Meghan hung the birdhouse from a tree branch.

_____ Meghan took the birdhouse out of the box.

The San Diego Zoo

The San Diego Zoo is one of the most impressive zoos in the world. This 100-acre zoo is home to over 4 thousand animals, including rare giant pandas, koalas, polar bears, hippos, and monkeys. Rather than living in cages, most animals in the San Diego Zoo live in areas that look and feel like their natural surroundings in the wild. Some special areas of the zoo include Tiger River, Sun Bear Forest, and Polar Bear Plunge. The mild climate of San Diego allows most animals to spend a great deal of time outdoors.

Fill in the blanks to the clues below. Write the answers in the puzzle.

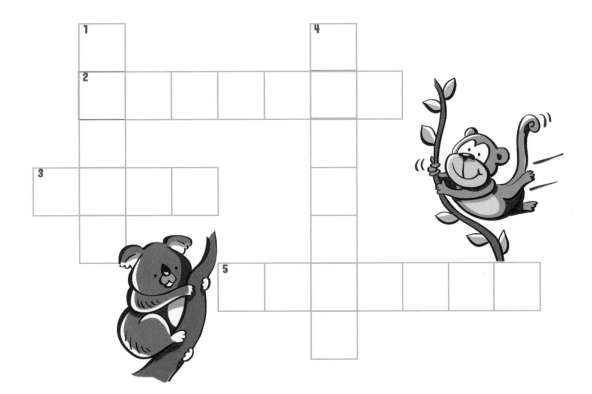

DOWN

1. Most animals in the San Diego Zoo do not live in

   _____.

4. The mild _____ of San Diego allows
   animals to enjoy time outdoors.

ACROSS

2. The San Diego Zoo is home to over 4 thousand _____.

3. Sun _____ Forest is a special area at the
   San Diego Zoo.

5. Most areas of the San Diego Zoo look and feel like

   the animals' _____ surroundings.

Using the Library

Libraries are buildings that hold thousands of books. If you have a library card, you can borrow a book from the library for free! After you check out the book you would like to borrow, you can take it home to read. It is important to take good care of the book that you borrow and return it in good condition. When you do this, other people will be able to enjoy the book after you have finished reading it.

Number the events in order.

_____ Check out a book from the library.

_____ Return the book to the library.

_____ Get a library card from the library.

_____ Take the book home to read.

_____ Take good care of the book.

Discovering Dinosaurs

Dinosaurs are animals that roamed Earth long ago. By looking at the different bones that have been found, we can tell that dinosaurs came in a variety of shapes and sizes. Some dinosaurs were plant-eaters, or herbivores. Other dinosaurs were meat-eaters, or carnivores. Dinosaurs that ate plants had flat teeth, while dinosaurs that ate meat had sharp teeth. Scientists continue to learn more about dinosaurs every time new dinosaur bones are found buried beneath the ground.

Answer the questions.

1. What does looking at the different dinosaur bones tell us?

   _____

   _____

2. What is another name for a plant-eater?

   _____

3. What is another name for a meat-eater?

   _____

4. How can you tell whether a dinosaur was a meat-eater or a plant-eater?

   _____

   _____

5. How do scientists learn more about dinosaurs?

   _____

   _____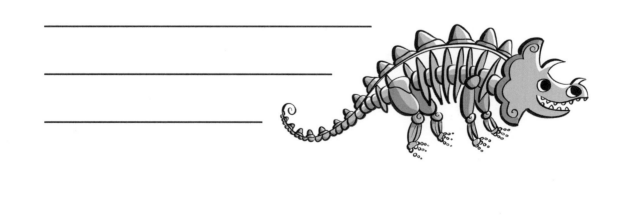

   _____

Chew on This!

Do you like to chew gum? If you lived in Singapore, your gum-chewing habit could get you into trouble with the law. In 1992, due to the mess created by gum stuck to sidewalks, posts, and underneath tables, the Singapore government passed a law that banned the sale of gum. Just recently, however, the government has decided to allow the sale of sugarless gum, but people who want to buy the gum must have a note from a doctor or dentist!

Answer the questions.

1. What country banned the sale of chewing gum?

_____

2. In what year was the sale of chewing gum banned?

_____

3. Where were people sticking gum?

_____

_____

4. What kind of gum is now allowed in Singapore?

_____

5. What must you have to buy gum in Singapore?

_____

Race to the Finish

Jamal knelt down at the starting line with the other runners. He looked ahead to the finish line, ready to run the race of his life. Suddenly, Jamal heard the sound of the starting gun. He pushed off from the ground and began to run. He pumped his arms and moved his legs as fast as they could go. As he neared the finish line, Jamal used a final burst of energy to race ahead of the other runners. He felt the ribbon pull across his chest. The crowd roared with applause and cheers. Jamal had won the race!

Number the events in the order in which they happened.

_____ Jamal used all of his energy to race ahead of the other runners.

_____ Jamal knelt at the starting line.

_____ Jamal ran as fast as he could.

_____ Jamal won the race!

_____ Jamal heard the sound of the starting gun.

Page 5

Down:
1. pajamas
4. bacon

Across:
2. upstairs
3. family
5. Saturday

Page 7

1. Answers will vary.
2. Answers will vary.
3. It lets them know you care.

Page 9

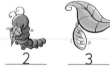

Page 11

1. False
2. True
3. False
4. True
5. True

Page 13

1. Mandy was very excited.
2. Pictures of shoes, clothes, toothbrush, and stuffed elephant should be circled.

Page 15

4 Sarah put the worm onto the hook.
3 The worm wiggled to get free.
6 Sarah waited to catch a fish.
1 Sarah opened the can of worms.
5 Sarah cast her line into the pond.
2 Sarah lifted the worm out of the can.

Page 17

Down:
1. helmet
4. traffic

Across:
2. safety
3. hurt
5. seatbelt

Page 19

1. "to fold paper"
2. birds, flowers, or fish
3. square pieces of paper
4. Japanese culture

Page 21

1. campfire
2. stick
3. roast
4. chocolate
5. some more

Page 23

1. northern border
2. 6 quadrillion gallons
3. Word Search:

Page 25

Page 27

1. The President of the United States and the First Family
2. 1600 Pennsylvania Avenue
3. 35 bathrooms
4. John Adams
5. the Executive Mansion or the President's Palace

Page 29

3 Pass the second beanbag from one hand to the other.
1 Hold 1 beanbag in each hand.
2 Toss 1 beanbag in a high arch toward the other hand.
5 Add a third beanbag.
4 Catch the first beanbag with your free hand.

Page 31

1. False
2. True
3. False
4. True
5. False

Page 33

1. Great Britain
2. 1840
3. Henry Cole
4. A Merry Christmas and a Happy New Year to You
5. Answers will vary.

Page 35

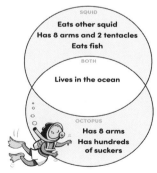

Page 37
1. It means a person cannot hear.
2. American Sign Language
3. She uses her hands to sign.
4. She is very fast.

Page 39
1. False
2. False
3. True
4. False
5. True

Page 41
1. Answers will vary.
2. They eat, sleep, and exercise.
3. They take their hats and gear.
4. They use fire hoses and extinguishers.

Page 43

Down:
1. people
4. school

Across:
2. help
3. doctors
5. advice

Page 45
1. light
2. water
3. split
4. red

Page 47
1. in New York City
2. a carved Roman coffin
3. nearly 3 million
4. the Met

Page 49
1. at the community pool
2. Monday and Wednesday afternoons
3. backstroke, crawl, and sidestroke
4. He will jump off the diving board.
5. No. He enjoys swimming now.

Page 51
4 Meghan put birdseed in the house.
1 Meghan bought a birdhouse from the store.
5 Meghan sat on the porch and waited for the birds.
3 Meghan hung the birdhouse from a tree branch.
2 Meghan took the birdhouse out of the box.

Page 53

Down:
1. cages
4. climate

Across:
2. animals
3. Bear
5. natural

Page 55
2 Check out a book from the library.
5 Return the book to the library.
1 Get a library card from the library.
3 Take the book home to read.
4 Take good care of the book.

Page 57
1. Dinosaurs came in all shapes and sizes.
2. herbivore
3. carnivore
4. A meat-eater has sharp teeth; a plant-eater has flat teeth.
5. They study dinosaur bones that are found beneath the ground.

Page 59
1. Singapore
2. 1992
3. on sidewalks, on posts, and underneath tables
4. sugarless
5. a doctor's or dentist's note

Page 61
4 Jamal used all of his energy to race ahead of the other runners.
1 Jamal knelt at the starting line.
3 Jamal ran as fast as he could.
5 Jamal won the race!
2 Jamal heard the sound of the starting gun.